I0468809

Discover Book Ideas

Kindle Niche Book Ideas That Sell Books, Make Writing Faster, and Create Best Sellers

Copyright © Dean R. Giles 2015

ISBN-13:
978-1530215461

ISBN-10:
1530215463

Legal Disclaimer

If you enjoy this book, please leave a review on Amazon.

(https://www.amazon.com/review/create-review?ie=UTF8&asin=B00IODSNVI)

Reviews help so much. Thank you in advance.

See my other books at Http://AustinsGift.com.

Have some feedback for me? Please send me an email, I love hearing from readers. dean@austinsgift.com

Dean R. Giles

Table of Contents

Introduction

Write in a Niche That Sells

"A journey of a thousand miles begins with a single step." -- Lao Tzu

The journey to writing a book that is popular begins with discovering a niche or topic that people are really interested in. That seems obvious, but few authors actually start where they need to. Just a little bit of research up front can explode sales on the back-end and make the writing worthwhile and fulfilling.

Self-publishing on Kindle has revolutionized the book market and has created opportunity for almost anyone to participate. However, there are few disappointments as deep as creating a book that doesn't sell. I know. I started there. I discovered how to do it wrong right out of the shoot. It took some diligent research and some hard knocks to finally get it right. This book is the starting point to endless possibilities that will actually bring results rather than disappointments.

There are a number of factors that go into a bestselling book on Amazon. Those factors come down to two important principles: discoverability and conversion. What I mean by these two are simply that the book has to have mechanisms that help it be "discovered" by the exact people who might buy it, and the second one means that it has to then appeal to them enough that they convert into paying customers and purchase the book.

I'm going to discuss the factors that create a book that is discoverable and that converts or sells. There are many of them, and I will touch on the most important ones, but I intend to show you how to easily discover the topics, niches, and titles that will have the best chances of making continual sales.

I am a firm believer in following working models, so I am going to show you how to find models that work, and show you examples of how to discover and mimic those models for your ultimate success.

I am a number one bestselling author. Below is a screen capture of one of my books during a time when it was a number one best seller for two Amazon categories.

Figure 1 Amazon Best Seller

I have written books that sell five or more copies per day, and I have written books that may sell one copy every other month.

I was frustrated that my first books really didn't sell well in spite of all of the personal time and money that I put into promoting them. I decided to do some real research, and have since read more than one hundred books, eBooks, courses, articles, and posts related to writing, publishing, and marketing books and eBooks. The methods that I developed from that research have changed my perspective about writing, but most of all have changed my success rate.

It is my hope and desire to save you the pain and frustration that I went through and help you to make your first book, and every book thereafter, a good selling asset and an endeavor worth pursuing. Writing has been very fulfilling to me. I love solving people's problems, and enjoy receiving email and comments from people who I have helped along the way.

After reading this eBook, if you feel like you have benefitted from these pages at all, I hope that you would share what you have learned with others. Let them know that they can also profit from writing if they approach it in a simple, straight forward, and systematic way. I will show you how easy that can really be and actually how much fun it can be.

Start With the End in Mind

This is truly the most important part of writing a book. What do you want to accomplish with writing a book? If you are hoping to sell your books to make some extra cash, then what topic will you choose to write about? What problems will you help people to solve? How will people find your book? Does a book on that topic really have a chance of being discovered and purchased by lots of people?

Chris Anderson, in his book, *The Long Tail*, explained that there is a market for almost anything, but the number of participants in that market gets fewer and fewer as the purchasers move away from the central products at the "big head" and glide towards the more specific products down the marketing tail.

Without trying to explain his entire book, I just want to relate some statistics to the above paragraph. Let's say that the most popular books on a certain subject make up 50% or more of all of the sales of books on that subject. Those books make up the "big head," and the percentages of sales drop off significantly as we get further and further away from that cluster of the most popular books.

What an author needs to do is to write about a topic that is so closely related to those most popular books, that their books are not very far away on the graph from the popular ones. They will want to discover a gap in the offerings that are available, and be able to fill that gap in a way that really meets customer needs and wants. Doing it in a creative way that brings out the writers own unique style and voice will create the magic that will sell your book. What I want to do with this book is to teach you how to find those "niche" topics that have a chance at really doing well and help you integrate those ideas into your writing.

Kindle Niches

I intend to focus on niches for Kindle eBooks for a number of reasons: I have had success with Kindle eBooks, Amazon will help you market them when they appear to be selling well, and because the markets for eBooks are exploding right now. The methods that I teach, however, can be used for discovering niches that would be good as niche websites, membership sites, ezine articles, Youtube videos, Udemy courses, or pretty much anything that requires niche type writing.

What is a Niche?

A niche is a market segmentation that is suitable or appropriate for a specific endeavor. In this case, there are general subjects or topics that are large and made up of several subtopics. The subtopics could then be broken down into several niches. These niches could be thought of as even smaller subtopics that are very specific. I'm going to be showing you what niches look like, how to recognize good ones, and how to kind of validate that they would do well as a Kindle eBook.

Niches from Bestsellers

Model success in all that you do.

Success breeds success, it is a true principle. People are judged by association, sometimes incorrectly, but often people tend to be like those that they associate with. You want your book to be successful by being associated with other successful books.

Signs of Success on Amazon

It may or may not seem obvious, but Amazon gives you lots of hints about what books are selling well that are associated with your interests, your buying habits, and your search habits. Amazon also has a number of lists that associate books. You really want your book associated with books that are selling well.

To find a niche, you need to deconstruct your search from the major topic to the subtopics and finally down to the very specific niches. There are so many ways to do this, and I will discuss many of those ways over the course of this book.

However, to set the stage for understanding how to get to the niches, I need you to select a major topic that you might have some interest in. It can be any topic. For this example, I am going to choose the topic of golf. I don't know this for a fact, but I believe that there are a lot of people who have an interest in golf, so I will pick that topic out of "thin air".

You need to find good topics to write about, but you can't spend a lot of time on researching the right topics, because you need to spend most of that time writing. This is how to do your research quickly. Get a paper and pencil out, or open a document where you are going to keep the ideas for niches as you run into them. I'm going to use a number of topics and niches as examples. You may not be interested in golf or any of the other subjects that I use as examples, but I want you to take time out to try these exercises with a subject that you are interested in, so simply have the tools ready so that you can write down niche ideas as you come across them.

Using the Kindle Store

The first thing that I am going to do is go to Amazon.com, and select the Kindle Store from the search bar. Then I am going to type golf in at the search bar, and then select "image", then finally click go.

Figure 2 Amazon Search

A page of books about golf will be displayed as shown in the figure below.

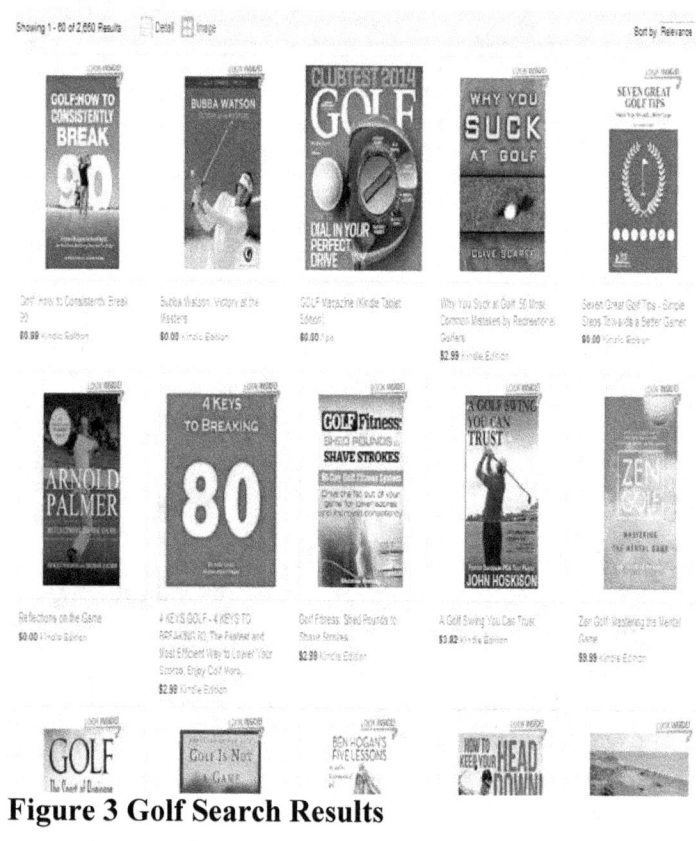

Figure 3 Golf Search Results

At the top of the screen you will see a message: "showing 1-60 of 2,650 results". This is definitely a broad topic that has a lot of interest. There could be many, many niches inside of this broad category.

It is important to note, however, that we haven't determined whether any of these books are selling.

That can be determined by clicking on the individual titles. If you take the first of the books that are not on free promotion and click on it, you will see the following in the product details section.

Product Details

File Size: 2900 KB

Print Length: 55 pages

Publisher: IGD Publishing (August 30, 2013)

Sold by: Amazon Digital Services, Inc.

Language: English

ASIN: B00EWU8OES

Text-to-Speech: Enabled

X-Ray: Not Enabled

Lending: Enabled

Amazon Best Sellers Rank: #36,889 Paid in Kindle Store (See Top 100 Paid in Kindle Store)
    #16 in Kindle Store > Kindle eBooks > Nonfiction > Sports > Golf
    #37 in Books > Sports & Outdoors > Golf

Figure 4 Amazon Best Seller Rank

Near the bottom of the screen the Amazon Best Seller Rank: #36,889 is displayed. This number represents where the book is relative to all other books selling on Amazon. It states that as far as sales go, it is selling better than all of the 2.5 million books on Amazon except for the 36,888 books that rank ahead of it. The ranks are recalculated often, and although they don't have a set conversion for how many copies of the book are being sold, the best seller rank can give you a rough idea of where the book stands.
A best seller rank of 50,000 produces, on average, between 1 and 3 sales per day.

Although the rank of 50,000 is somewhat arbitrary, it is one that I like to shoot for. I am looking for three or more eBooks that rank below 50,000 somewhere in the first 20 books listed. I am even more interested in a topic if it has one or two listed below the 20,000 range.

This list is for the broad category, however, we will want to narrow down the scope of our intended book even further than this. There are some great hints as to what those narrowed subtopics might look like.

Related Searches

At the top of the screen of figure 3, the screen produced by searching for our golf topic, there are a couple of links to "related" searches. There are two links, but the "goldfinch" link doesn't really apply to our topic. The other one, "golf instruction", does, and should be one of the next searches that we try.
The Golf Instruction search has fewer titles, but some of the titles sell even better than the general titles that we looked at previously.

Customers Who Bought This Also Bought

Right below the product description of each book is a section called "customers who bought this also bought". This section looks like the figure below:

Figure 5 Customers Who Bought This Item Also Bought

Here are some other books that might be better segmented into a subtopic. Whatever your topic of interest is, write down the titles of the books that come up that look interesting and are related to your topic.

Another source of bestselling book titles is BarnesAndNoble.com. Type in your topic name at the search bar on top. For this example I am going to use "be healthy" as my seed keyword or my broad topic.

Figure 6 Barnes And Noble Search

Notice all of the subtopics listed here: Diet, Exercise, Weight Loss, Healthy Eating. This is what I'm talking about. Taking the broader topic and dividing it up into smaller, more specific niches. Barnes and Noble also has a customers who bought this also bought section once you click into the individual books.

Here is what the product details look like on Barnes and Noble.

Product Details

ISBN-13: 9780743266420

Publisher: Free Press

Publication date: 6/28/2005

Pages: 352

Sales rank: 79,984

Product dimensions: 5.50 (w) x 8.40 (h) x 0.90 (d)

Figure 7 Barnes and Noble Sales Rank

Notice that it also has a sales rank. Barnes and Noble claims that its sales rank is developed over six months of sales information, so it may take some time to get a sales rank there, but it makes a great place to get ideas for topics to write about.

On Amazon and Barnes and Noble there is another way to get good book ideas. That is through the category selection. Open Amazon.com, select Kindle Store, then just click on go.

Department
Kindle Store
Kindle Devices (28)
Kindle Accessories (564)
Kindle Blogs (14,323)
Kindle eBooks (2,423,683)
Kindle Magazines (650)
Kindle Newspapers (175)
Kindle Singles (492)
Kindle Worlds (394)

Figure 8 Amazon Categories

From here click on Kindle eBooks. Look over the general categories and select one that is interesting to you. Below is a picture of what some of the categories look like. Notice the numbers in the parenthesis beside the categories. This number tells you the number of books in that category. Large numbers tell you that there is a lot of interest around the topic, but also says that there may be a lot of competition. I like large numbers, because I believe that I can come up with a narrow niche that uses the momentum of the number of people interested in the topic, but that I can select something specific enough to not really be in competition with any specific books in the list.

Validation

If you haven't taken the time yet. Open up Amazon.com and just do a few searches.

Enter broad topics that you are interested in. Don't look at any of the sales rankings yet—just write down the topics and books that come up that seem interesting to you.

Now go back and click on the first few books that interested you. What are the sales ranks of the books that you picked? If there are three that rank in the 50,000 and below, you probably have a good niche. Are any of them under 20,000? If so, you could have a "hot" niche. Hot niches have lots of potential, but can have so much competition, that your book won't be noticed.

Amazon and Barnes and Noble can be great places to find niches. For eBooks, you should always validate your niches at one of these online book stores. If you are going to publish to Kindle first, I would suggest that you always do an Amazon search with the title that you have in mind before you publish your book. Make sure that there are books that have a sales rank of 50,000 or less. That would insure that you have a topic that has very good sales potential. This would be your validation point.

Niches from the Learning Center

Now we start into the section about where to find a lot of really good niche book ideas very quickly. Those ideas still need to be validated against a search on Amazon—but below are the hot beds of inspiration that will help you find those book titles almost instantly.

Online education is growing field. With communication the way it is, there are so many opportunities to learn from people via courses that can be purchased online. There is an online community where a lot of courses are kept that people can buy or courses that they can take for free. That place is Udemy.com. Go to Udemy.com and type your topic into the search bar.

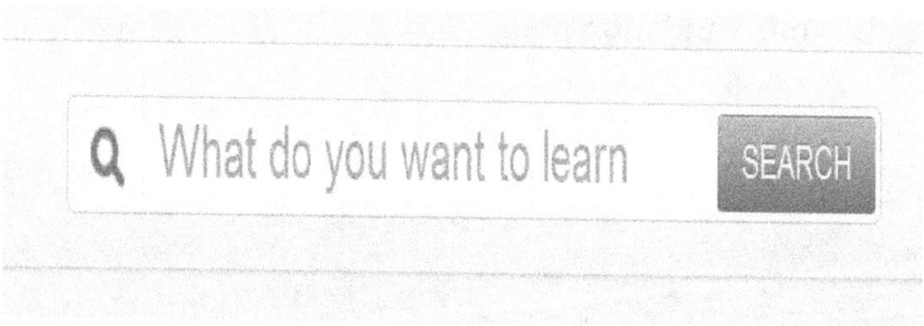

Figure 9 Udemy Classes

You will get a listing of classes. Sort the classes by popularity and on the price box select paid. For this example I am going to select "Microsoft" as my main category.

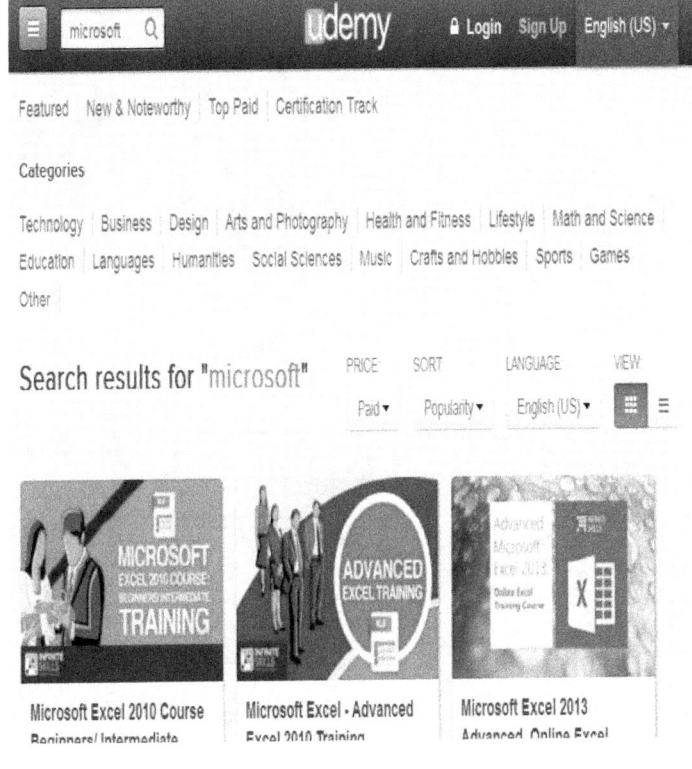

Figure 10 Udemy Catalogue

This is what the search results look like when searching by popularity and excluding the free classes. You want to write about subjects that people are already paying to learn about. It looks like Microsoft Excel grabs the top spots of this search. The screen shot below shows more of the search results.

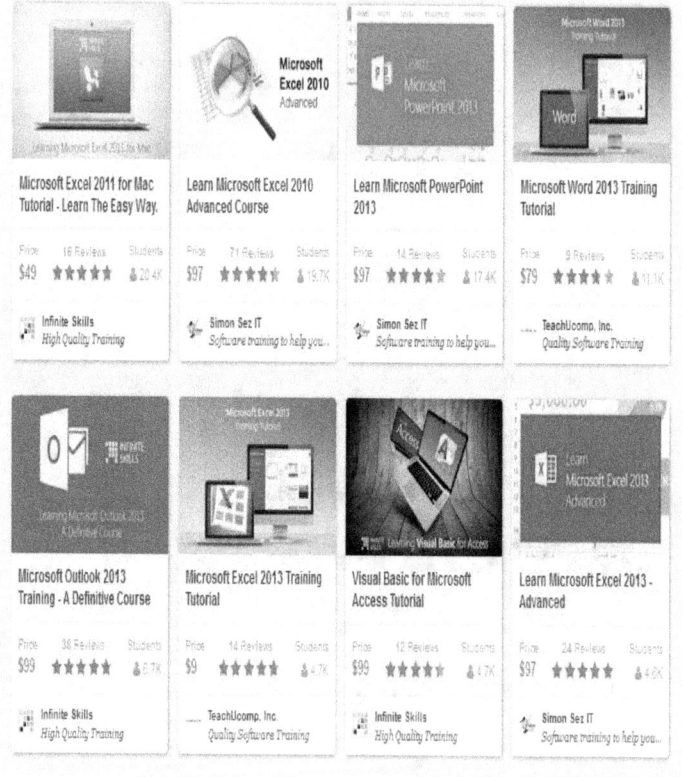

Figure 11 Specific Classes

Notice that there are a lot of subtopics here, Microsoft Power Point, Word, Outlook, and Visual Basic, along with more Excel classes, and there are 5 more pages of results.

If you refer back to figure 9, the first screenshot from Udemy, you will see that there are a number of main categories for classes, those categories include:

Udemy Categories

Technology
Business
Design
Arts and Photography
Health and Fitness
Lifestyle
Math and Science
Education
Languages
Humanities
Social Sciences
Music
Crafts and Hobbies
Sports
Games
And Other

Click on one of the categories and see what shows up. You might be surprised that many of the courses cost 99 dollars or more!

Each course represents a pretty good niche. Think about the ones that interest you. Which ones would you like to learn more about?

Now open up one or more of the courses. Inside the course is a table of contents or course curriculum, like the one below.

CURRICULUM

SECTION 1: FUNDAMENTALS

1	▶ Baking The Cake	⬇	07:36
2	▶ Removing Cakes From Pans . . .	⬇	01:49
3	▶ Decorating - Getting Started	⬇	04:07
4	▶ Decorator Bags	⬇	05:09
5	▶ Folding A Parchment Bag	⬇	01:48
6	▶ Decorator Tips	⬇	03:53
7	▶ Coloring The Buttercream Icing	⬇	02:03
8	▶ Borders	⬇	00:53
9	▶ Gerber Daisy Demonstration	.	02:40

Figure 12 Curriculum

Each of these items in the course curriculum could potentially be made into a book on its own, or you could combine three or four related items to create a book.

Do you see how easy finding niches can be? With Udemy, you know that people are paying for this information, so it validates that there is a market for this information.

Just Do It

Get out your paper or open the document that you are using for your personal research. Go to Udemy.com now. Look through the categories. Write down the categories that interest you. Write down the titles of the courses that catch your attention. Write down any ideas of better ways to write the title of the courses being offered.

Now open up a few of the classes, and write down the sections of the curriculum that interest you the most. You should be getting a number of items on your paper or in your research document.

Niches From New Tools and Apps Including Web 2.0

Technology is exploding. People interact in ways that they never used to. Social media, such as Facebook, Twitter, LinkedIn, and Pinterest take up a lot of bandwidth in people's lives. There are new gadgets, the iPad, iPod, iPhone, Blackberry, Android, Motorola, and on, and on. New game consoles and new games are coming out all of the time.

Google has a news station that can keep you abreast of the latest breaking news about new devices, new apps, and new games. Open up Google.com, from the search page put in any search term. Once the search results are up, select News instead of Web. Then enter new devices, new apps, or new games. The results will look like this:

Google | new devices | 🔍

Web   Images   **News**   Shopping   Videos   More ▾   Search tools

About 14,300,000 results (0.72 seconds)

New medical device group seeks to cut red tape
Tech Page One - 9 hours ago
Manufacturers who design and test **new** medical **devices** have long complained of the complicated approval process, a time-chewing and ...

Apple iPhone 6 Rumors: Apple Making New Mid-Level Device ...
International Business Times - 3 hours ago
The report confirms that Apple is producing two **new devices**, presumably two new versions of the iPhone 6, one with a 4.7 inch screen and ...

Rumor: Apple working on 4.7", 5.6" iPhones for release in Q3 2014
Apple Insider - 12 hours ago

Explore in depth (30 more articles)

Figure 13 New Devices

These stories will usually revolve around devices that are new, or ones that will be new when they come out. When you read about a new device that isn't released yet, write down the name of the device. Create a Google Alert, you can do that here http://www.google.com/alerts .

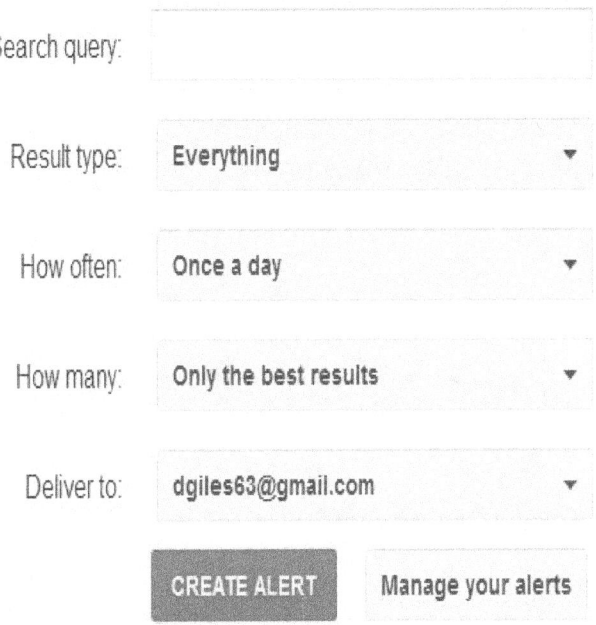

Figure 14 Google Alerts

Set the alert for some specific keyword, like the name of the new device. Now every time Google comes across a new article on the new device, Google will send you an email and a link to the article. You can keep on top of the breaking news for that device or app. Timing is everything with this strategy.

Try to time the release of your book to co-inside with the release of the new device or app. The book should sell very well indeed.

When Google discontinued their Keyword Tool, and introduced their new Keyword Planner, I used this strategy to create a book about the new tool. It taught the basics about the tool and how to use a couple of the new features in ways that you couldn't use the old tool. The book was a huge success and became the #1 Bestseller in two categories. You can see my book here on Amazon.
http://www.amazon.com/dp/B00E45ADKE/ .

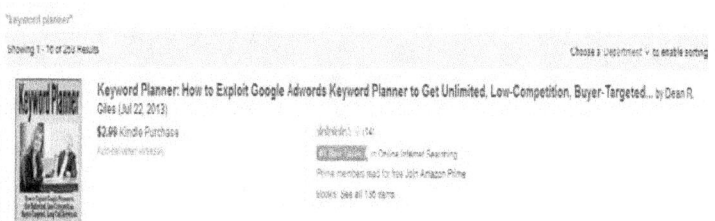

Figure 15 Best Seller

The only drawback to this approach is that technology changes and you will have to update your book on a regular basis. There is also the problem that the new technology becomes old, and people stop using it, or the devices, apps, or games are replaced by something else. Your book would stop selling altogether then.

But, the possibilities of having a hot selling book for a while is very high, and the timing might make it so that your book is the first one out there.

Don't shy away from these niches because they may not be as long lasting as others, there is still a lot of money to be made in these new technology types of environments.

Jot It Down

OK. It is time to practice. Just take out your paper or open your document of research ideas. Open up Google.com, Click on News and type in New Devices, New Apps, New Games, or anything else you might be interested in. Now write down the ones that jump out at you. You should be accumulating some really good niche book ideas.

Niches from Tough Problems

People experience problems every day. People experience pain, anxiety, and discomfort from these problems. People will pay a lot of money to find relief from the pain of the problems that they are facing every day. I love writing books that solve people's problems. I love to hear about lives that are changed and people who have found relief because of the solutions that I have offered in books and/or articles that I have written.

Many of the best books that I have read have been one problem—one solution types of books. They are laser-focused on one specific problem and they deliver an actionable method for solving the problem that they have identified. I like these kinds of books because they are right-to-the-point, they usually deliver exactly what they promise, and they usually do it in a simple, efficient way so that I can implement the solution that they propose.

There are a number of tools and resource that you can use to identify these problems. One of the best, and easiest to use is the Stack Exchange. You can access the stack exchange here. http://stackexchange.com/sites# . Here is what you will see at the Stack Exchange.

Figure 16 Stack Exchange

There are a number of links to explore, but I like to go right to the Icon View, shown below:

Figure 17 Stack Exchange Icon View

Notice that the icons are different sizes. The size represents the size of the site that they point to.

Each site is an authority site which has a constant stream of questions and answers going on around the subject of the site.

The Stake Exchange site is really pretty simple. Anyone can ask a question, anyone can answer the question, answers are voted on, and the best answers bubble to the top.

Here is a screen shot of how to use any of the Stack Exchange sites:

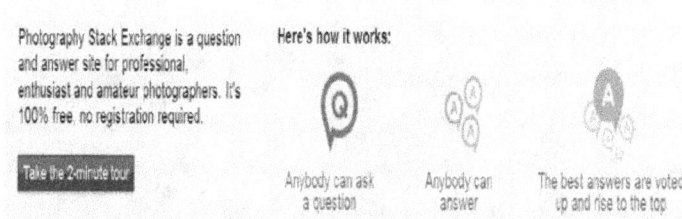

Figure 18 How to Use Stack Exchange

This is what the site looks like with questions and answers.

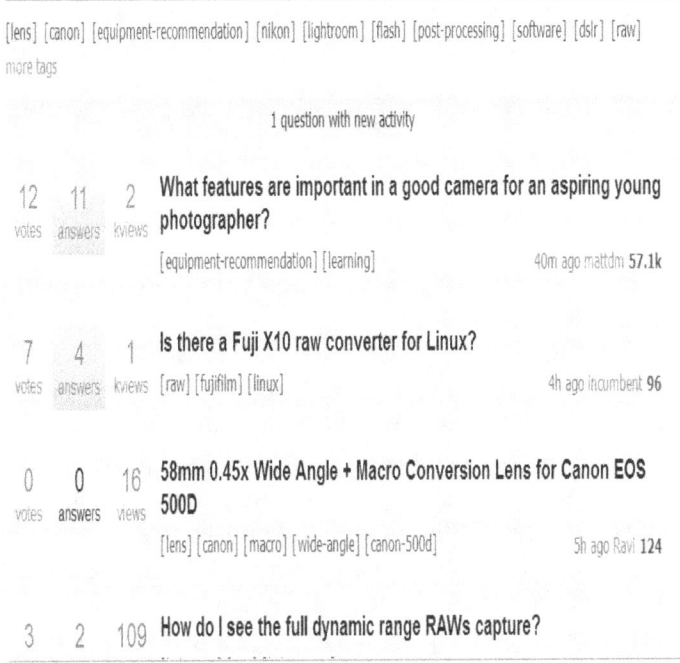

Explore Our Questions

[lens] [canon] [equipment-recommendation] [nikon] [lightroom] [flash] [post-processing] [software] [dslr] [raw]
more tags

1 question with new activity

12 votes | 11 answers | 2 kviews | **What features are important in a good camera for an aspiring young photographer?**
[equipment-recommendation] [learning]
40m ago mattdm **57.1k**

7 votes | 4 answers | 1 kviews | **Is there a Fuji X10 raw converter for Linux?**
[raw] [fujifilm] [linux]
4h ago incumbent **96**

0 votes | 0 answers | 16 views | **58mm 0.45x Wide Angle + Macro Conversion Lens for Canon EOS 500D**
[lens] [canon] [macro] [wide-angle] [canon-500d]
5h ago Ravi **124**

3 | 2 | 109 | **How do I see the full dynamic range RAWs capture?**

Figure 19 Questions and Answers

This is one of my FAVORITE places to collect information for my books. There are both professionals and amateurs that visit these sites. The questions help me to know what people are interested in, and I have even asked some questions myself that have been answered very well by people on these sites.

Notice that there are tags at the top of the screen shot. You can immediately pop to questions about the most popular topics simply by clicking on the tabs.

Put It into Practice

Ok. Take out your paper or open your document with your book ideas. Go to http://stackexchange.com/sites# . Look over the page of icons that represent the categories that you can browse. Write down the categories that seem interesting to you. Now open up a few of those categories and read some of the questions. Are any of those questions interesting enough to write a book on? What if you combined several of those questions? Look at the tabs at the top of the page. Write down the most interesting ones. Click on a few of the tabs or on the more tabs button. Write down any other interesting questions your run into. Your document should be more than a couple of pages by now. If not, don't despair, I have more ways of coming up with those niches in the methods that follow.

Niches from Professionals

What if there were a large group of professionals that collaborate together and help each other through difficult problems in their profession, or simply chat about life around some career? What if you could be a fly on the wall, and listen to their conversations? Do you think that you could come up with great material for a book?

Well, such a place exists in cyberspace. It is called LinkedIn. LinkedIn is a place to post your professional profile, which is something that you have to do to really be a member. Once you are a member you can ask to join groups on LinkedIn. Go to http://linkedin.com to check it out.

Linked in.

Be great a

Figure 20 LinkeIn

After becoming a member and filling out your profile, then you can ask to join the groups on LinkedIn. There are two types of groups, public and private. You can search the groups by selecting groups from the drop down next to the search bar, and by typing in the name of your broad topic. The public groups have a "view" button, and the private groups have a "join" button, as shown below:

Figure 21 LinkedIn groups

These groups have working professionals that are members of the group. When you make a request to join a group, if the moderator asks you why you want to join the group, mention that you are writing a book and have a great interest in the topic of the group. Usually the moderator will let you join, but some may not.

LinkeIn also has ways to link up with other professionals, it allows you to follow companies, and get news about industries. LinkedIn is another source of great information that can help you fill your books and answer questions about most any field.

Your Turn

OK. Now go out to LinkedIn.com, if you don't already have an account, open one up and fill out a few of the fields. Select a group or two to join. Join a new group every couple of weeks. Pretty soon you should have a good basis for gathering information from professionals for a book on any interest of yours.

Niches from Hot and Popular Topics

What are the hot and popular topics today? Perhaps that is a loaded question. What topics do you hear about over and over again on the news? Those would be great topics to explore and look for niches to write about.

If there is someone who personifies the current hot and popular topics it is Oprah Winfrey. If it isn't a popular topic, and Oprah talks about it, then it becomes a popular topic. Oprah has her own network, and it is easy to skim the network for popular topics. See the screenshot of the webpage below:

Figure 22 The Oprah Winfrey Network

There are a number of ways to look at the shows and the topics on the site that are being highlighted. You can search the upcoming schedule and look for the names of people that Oprah will be interviewing, look for the topics that will be discussed.

One interesting one that I found was this one:

Figure 23 Hot Topics

Oprah created a brand new word, "colorism". My guess is that it will become more and more popular, as it is brought up again and again on her show and in other places.

It may make a good topic for a book, and someone writing on it now could have the first book out there about this topic.

There are a number of other experts that can make a topic popular just by featuring it on their show. A number of them also get some time on the Oprah Winfrey Network (OWN). Those people include Dr. Phil, Dr. Oz, and a whole list of others featured on Oprah's Daily Lessons as shown below:

Daily Life Lessons

The one thing every estranged father needs to do to reconnect

Dr. Phil's "Sweet 16" rules for winning in the real world

Can single mothers teach their sons how to be men?

Find your emotional balance

Iyanla Vanzant counsels a man who left his family

How to discover your deepest-held belief

Figure 24 People That Make Topics Popular

The hot topics may be subjects that resurge again and again, or may be ones that flair up and are gone.

The risk is higher writing books about hot topics and fads, because interest in those thing wax then wane, but there can be some good money in books about those topics. The topics can come back after a time of almost dormancy, and they can be combined with other topics to round out a book. The beauty of these topics is that they are hot at the moment simply because they were touched on by some very popular Icon.

Hands-On Time

Here it is again. Take time now to go to http://www.oprah.com/own . Get your paper or open the document where you have been taking your notes on topics and niches that you might consider writing about.

Write down any broad categories that you might see on the page. Click on different tabs and see what other categories and topics come up. What things jump out at you? How does Oprah use controversy or contrarian views in the topics that she chooses? Why are some of these topics hot right now?

Click on some of the shows or episodes. What topics do you see discussed there that might interest you? Could you make possible book titles out of those topics? Are there related topics that could be combined or expanded on?

Niches from Hobbies

Everyone has hobbies and interests. I like chess, scrapbooking, family activities, and science fiction/fantasy books. You find out the most about a person when you find out what they do during those moments when they don't have to be doing anything. Some of the world's greatest passions are built around interests and hobbies. People interested in a specific interest or hobby rarely buy just one book about it, they buy a book and later buy another one. Pretty soon they have a library of books on the subjects that really interest them. That is why hobbies can be such lucrative book markets.

Wikipedia has a huge list of hobbies, you can see it at http://en.wikipedia.org/wiki/List_of_hobbies . The list is segregated into the following categories:

WIKIPEDIA
The Free Encyclopedia

List of hobbies

From Wikipedia, the free encyclopedia

This is a partial **list of hobbies**. A hobby typically done during one's leisure time. T have organized membership association

Contents [hide]

Main page
Contents
Featured content
Current events
Random article
Donate to Wikipedia
Wikimedia Shop

▼ Interaction
Help
About Wikipedia
Community portal
Recent changes
Contact page

▶ Tools

▶ Print/export

Figure 23 Wikipedia Hobbies

Wikipedia can also be a great place to come up with other book ideas. It has references to most any subject. The information found in Wikipedia is usually very general, although it can help you with the basics, you will need much more specific information for your books. But, Wikipedia can be a good place to start, and an excellent place to find the subtopics that can make great niches to write about.

Once you have your basic hobby that you are interested in, you could browse the topics in Wikipedia looking for questions regarding the topic or specifics that are much narrower than the Wikipedia categories.

Here is a screen shot of a tiny fraction of the list of hobbies:

Indoors [edit]

- 3D Printing
- Animal fancying
- Amateur radio[1]
- Audiophilia
- Baton twirling
- Bboying
- Blogging
- Chainmail making
- Coloring
- Computer programming
- Conlanging
- Cooking
- Cosplaying
- Creative writing
- Crocheting
- Dance
- Digital Arts
- Drama
- Drawing
- Embroidery
- Fantasy Sports
- Fishkeeping

Figure 24 Hobbies on Wikipedia

Notice that most hobbies are blue links to other
Wikipedia pages. You can take the name of the
hobbies and put them into Google. Also search for the
name of the hobbies on Amazon. You will begin to
find more and more information about those hobbies.
Finding specific niches should become easy with this
much information about them. Most hobbies will
have authority web sites that discuss them and will
have forums about them.

To find the forums or blogs about hobbies that you
are interested in, simply type the name of the hobby
into Google and type forum after the name. If you are
interested in blogs about the subject, simply type in
Google the name of the hobby followed by the word
blog.

Exercises

OK. Time for some personal practice. Open up
http://en.wikipedia.org/wiki/List_of_hobbies. Click
on a few hobbies that interest you. Take out your
paper with topic ideas on it or open up your electronic
document. Write down the major topics and any niche
ideas that jump out at you as you read about the
hobbies. Follow the links in Wikipedia and write
down any questions that come to mind.

Niches Around Pets

Pets can be found everywhere. People love animals, but don't always like some of their behaviors. They also need lots information about how to care for their animals, what to feed them, and what to expect from the animals.

Pets are among some of the best subjects to write about, especially if you are a pet owner and have had good experiences with pets.

Facebook has some great pet groups, some of those groups are very specific. Search by breed of dog or specific pets. The groups on Facebook often have discussions about their pets. Watch for questions and answers that could make really good niches for possible books.

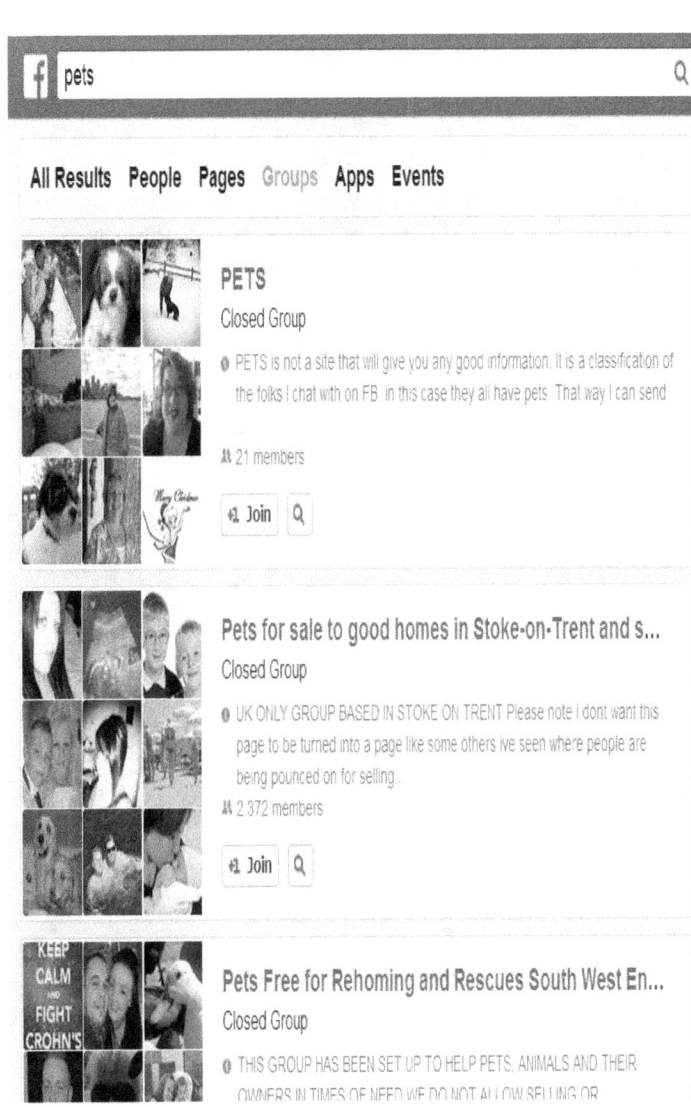

Figure 25 Pet Groups on Facebook

Get It on Your List

OK. It is practical experience time again. Get out your paper or open your document that is becoming filled with book ideas. Open up a Facebook pet group and write down the main topics that might interest you and any topics you might want to research further. Join the ones that seem interesting to you. Interact with the groups and add to the conversations. You will be amazed at how many people want to share their stories and experiences related to their pets.

Niches Around Sports

Every aspect of sports provides opportunities for niche books. There are books about how to play the sport, how to teach children the sport, how to buy equipment for the sport, about sports teams and sports personalities.

Have you ever heard the words "sports fan", fan is short for fanatic. Sports are big around the world and most everyone has a sport that they are interested in.

A good place for a little sports history is the Sports Encyclopedia, http://www.sportsecyclopedia.com/ . Google, the television news channels, and most newspapers have daily articles about sports and sports teams. Dig in. Look for interesting questions about sports, sports teams, or particular players. Sports has a lot of good niche books already out there, and there is plenty of room for many, many more.

Putting It to Practice

Go ahead and pull out the paper with your list of niche ideas or open up the document where you have been keeping them. Make your way out to Wikipedia, Facebook Groups or Sports Encyclopedia and write down any topics, niches, or titles that interest you.

What jumps out at you and why? What concerns do you see around sports? Injuries, children consumed by the sport or parents that push too hard? There are so many topics around sports that people would be interested in. Jot down the ones that pique your interest.

What Sells and Why?

When it comes to putting out a book that people will buy there are two important concepts. One is discoverability and the other is conversion. You may have the world's greatest book, but if no one knows about it, you won't get any sales. The other is what leads people to buy the book after they have discovered it. Both of these things fall within the realm of marketing.

In the good old days, authors were picked up by publishers. The publisher spent the time and money needed to try and get the book discovered and marketed. In this new era of self-publishing, the responsibility for marketing the book falls to the author.

The book *Author, Publisher, Entrepreneur* (APE), delves deeper into the hard fact that, as an author you are everything to your book. Another book that I found helpful around this subject was *Write. Publish. Repeat.* The authors of that book touched on how to market without feeling sullied by the marketing. There is no getting around it. In order to "help" Amazon sell your book, you are going to have to do some marketing. I'm going to outline some fundamentals and give you what you need to make the marketing easier—but there are whole books that are written just around eBook marketing, and I would suggest that you continue your education reading even further about book marketing.

How to Help Amazon Help You

Amazon wants to make you and your book successful. It is amazing what Amazon will do for you when your book is making sales. It is also amazing what they won't do for you when your book is not selling.

So, the bottom line is that Amazon helps those who help themselves. I'm going to discuss a number of factors that make your book discoverable, or prevent it from being discovered.

Discovering Your Book

How will your book be discovered on Amazon? The premise of this book is that writing in the right niches will increase the chances that your book will be seen. However, that won't be the case if you don't get the right words and phrases into your title, description, search terms, and find the right categories.

Your Book Title

This may be one of the most important decisions that you make. A title has to grab attention, set expectations for the book, engage browsers, and ultimately convince prospects to become customers.

If that weren't enough, you have to do it in few enough words that the title can still be read in a postage stamp size cover picture. Among the secrets of a good title is to break it up. Set the title as a few words that stand out, then the subtitle as a longer, more descriptive, and more detailed and wordy sentence.

Open up a browser to Amazon.com, type in a broad topic such as health, wealth, or pets, any type of word that will bring up a number of non-fiction books. Note that almost all of them follow this example. Title, subtitle. The title is written in big letters and stands out. It is easy to read and see on the cover. The subtitle will be in small print, or will not be on the cover itself.

The title could be a broad term or phrase found using the Google Keyword Planner. The book could be differentiated by the subtitle alone.

Once you have your niche topic selected, and have some good ideas about what to put in your book, then it is time to start thinking about the title.

Take your list of ideas and begin working with them for a good title. Write down five to seven versions of what you think the title could be. Now open up Amazon.com, select the Kindle Store, and type in the first proposed title.

Is there already a book or books with the exact name? What is the sales rank of that book? Is it below the 50,000 sales rank mark? Is it below the 20,000 sales rank mark? You might want to keep some elements of that title, but make sure the subtitle is significantly different.

There are other things to look at, when you start typing your proposed book's name in the Amazon search bar. As you type, Amazon makes suggestions for you.

This is what the Amazon Suggestion box looks like:

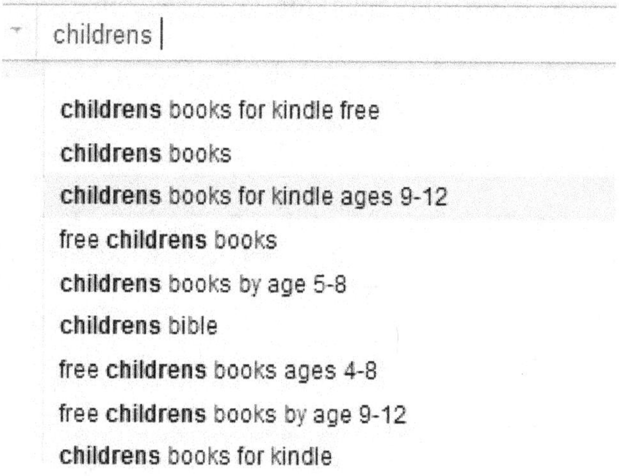

Figure 26 Amazon Suggestions

Are the first two words or so of your title already among the suggestions? This could make a big difference in your book being discovered. If there is a term that is in the drop down that is close to the proposed title of your book, could you use this term in the title of your book?

Write down a number of these drop down terms from the search box. They might make good search terms for your book.

Make Your Book Title Memorable

Now that you have experimented with a few book titles, can you add a word or two to the drop down phrase that you found that will capture people's attention, that will raise eye brows, or make people wonder? That is the kind of title magic that will get clicks for your book.

Keywords to Find Your Book

When people type a term or phrase into the Amazon search box, you would really like them to see your book in the results. The only way they have a chance of seeing your book in the result is if the term or phrase that they typed in is included in:

Your title (including subtitles), the series name, the seven search terms that Amazon allows you to specify for your book, the categories, or the description.

We have talked a lot about your title and about choosing topics that people are interested in. The rubber meets the road here where you are choosing your terms that you want people to use to find your book. Remember that you want to choose terms that have a lot of search traffic. Amazon doesn't give you any statistics about its search traffic. The keyword suggestion is one of the few hints that Amazon gives you about what terms are being typed into the Amazon search bar. You can use Googles Keyword Planner, but the audience will be different on Amazon.

I suggest that you also look at the sales rank of the books that come up when you type in a search phrase that you might be considering for your book. I want you to be "successful by association." If you find a phrase that brings up books with sales ranks under 20,000, then use that phrase as one of your seven search phrases, because you want your book to be seen with that crowd, and to sell like those books sell.

Conversion

What is going to push the people browsing books into actually making a purchase? Your book has to have a purpose, it has to solve a problem, answer a question, and pique interest and curiosity.

The title has to covey the benefits of reading the book. There is a delicate balance between using search phrases in the title to get more people to see your book and in the words used to entice those same people to actually click on the title or to buy the book.

I have read that the title and the cover simply have to get people to click on the icon so that they go one step deeper. The book description and the "look inside" feature have to do the next bit of selling.

The Cover Story

Your cover has to tell a story. It has to look good at full size, at medium size, and at thumbnail size. The cover has to catch people's attention. It has to say, "Click Me!"

I would suggest that you pull up a number of books around your topic and look for the most common features of the successful books.

If most of the books in your category have a picture of a boy and a dog on the front—then at least consider having a boy and a dog on your cover.

The other tactic that works well is to do the exact opposite. If your category is littered with "look-a-likes" then choose something totally different and off the wall. Let your customers know right away why they don't want another look-a-like book and how your book is different and will definitely do more for them.

The cover is so important you may want to consider having a professional do the cover. You can find contractors that will do your cover at a reasonable price. Fiverr.com, Odesk.com, Elance.com all have good cover designers and prices can start at five dollars. NOTE: Be sure to sort the potential cover designers by rating. Pick one of the highest rated designers for the best results. The best results will be achieved if you can supply the cover picture that you want, explain how you want your cover to look, and supply a link to cover picture on Amazon that the designer can use a s a model.

The Book Description

Tell them what they will get from reading your book. What are the overall benefits?

Tell a story that can help your perspective readers identify with your book, then tell them how you will solve their problem with your book. You have about 800 words to do this in the book description. Use at least 500 words here.

The Look-Inside Feature

Amazon provides about ten percent of your book as a sample for readers to look at. Make it the best 10 percent of your book. Spend a little time here explaining why they need the book and introducing the most important parts of your book.

Making the Writing Fun and Easy

Write about what you love. There is a saying, "write what you know." You don't have to be an expert, in fact, sometimes it helps to share with other people how you went from knowing nothing about the topic to being proficient with it. But, in my opinion, you have to be passionate.

Personal Inventory

People have asked me why I didn't start with this section. There is a good reason. Everyone needs ideas about what topics to write about. First and foremost I wanted to open your mind to all of the possibilities and all of the absolutely successful topics that others have found. Now that you have the skills to recognize opportunity, you finally have the tools to look inside yourself at the most fertile fields of book ideas possible, those topics that you already know a little bit about and have an interest in.

When you write about your own experiences and your own feelings the writing is easy and it flows seamlessly from one thing to the next. If writing is like going to the dentist, then you are doing it wrong!

Before you start your first book or your next book, take a moment to create a personal inventory. This is going to help you come up with the right ideas concerning what you can write about. Do the inventory first, then apply the concepts of delving into niches and categories.

What Interests Do You Have?

Have you ever read a book where the author really didn't seem to have a huge interest in the subject? Sure, they covered the topics, but they lacked real passion in their presentation. I have read a lot of those kinds of books, and frankly, never want to read another one as long as I live!

I have presented the concept that doing some research about the topic and niche to see if it will be profitable is important, but it is equally important to choose a topic that you have a great interest in. If you have an interest in the topic, it is so much more likely that the topic will be easier for you to write about—but more importantly, people will feel your enthusiasm for the topic and will love your book.

If you don't have that enthusiasm for your topic, even if you are able to finish your book, which becomes much more difficult indeed, it is likely that it won't garner a lot of sales.

I have read short eBooks of 10 pages or less that delivered on actionable steps and lots of enthusiasm, and have felt they were so much more valuable than long books of hundreds of pages that delivered a lot of information, but not much that I felt I could use, and no encouragement to really get out and use it. If there were a secret to writing books that people love, it would be to write about a subject that you are truly passionate about—your enthusiasm will shine through, and be mesmerizing.

What Hobbies Do You Enjoy?

Make a list of your hobbies. Do you like arts and crafts? Have you ever had even a brief exposure to painting, sculpting, knitting, or scrapbooking? Each of those types of creation have a market and a following. Have you ever collected model trains, planes, Lego sets, or matchbox cars? There are active hobbyists that are absolute fanatics about those and other collectibles. Do you play chess, golf, tennis, or racquetball? There are a lot of other people with those same hobbies. They are anxious to learn new things and to improve their games.

If you have an interest in any number of hobbies, there are markets for most of them, and lots of people that follow those hobbies.

What Problems Have You Dealt With?

I have read loads of books dealing with real and difficult problems and issues. Almost everyone wrestles with being over-weight a little bit. Most people battle with self-confidence and motivation. We all have goals and dreams, but lack the skills, the confidence, and the motivation to do anything about it. Most people have the desire to eat better, to build muscle, to improve their looks, and to feel better about themselves. We all have the desire to do something about it, but, again, need some help getting there.

Perhaps you have dealt with disappointment in life, maybe you have struggled with a disability, or been associated with someone who has. Perhaps you have dealt with depression, anxiety, or other intense stresses in life. Maybe you have struggled through bankruptcy, repeated lay-offs, or unreliable employment.

What Jobs Have You Had, or Have You Ever Been Unemployed?

Most jobs require some specialized skills. What makes you better at your job than other people? What are the most important aspects of what you do? What would you teach someone just beginning in your career?

If you have ever been unemployed—employment books, resume writing, and books that deal with social media such as LinkedIn are all on the uptake right now and very popular.

What Problems Do People Come to You to Solve?

You have valuable information. People come to you often to get it. What is it that people come to you for your advice about? How do you save money? How do you have harmony in your home? What parenting advice could you give? What issues have you helped people to overcome? What diets have you tried? How do you balance nutrition and speed of fixing meals and juggling everyday activities? What decisions have helped you in life and which ones have got in your way and caused you pain? What could you teach someone that would change their life and make them a better person? What would you teach your children if you had one chance to talk to them and had their full attention?

Write It All Down

Take out your paper or open your document with book ideas. Create a section for Personal Inventory. Write down the answers to some of the questions above. Write down the broad categories that you would love to write about.

Now try to balance the needs. Find a topic that has lots of interest, and could be a topic that aligns with your personal inventory. Write the book that you would love to read! Write the book that solves the biggest problem for everyone like you!

One thing to stay away from—don't write a book about a general topic, there are too many of those, they don't sell well, it takes too long to finish, and people get bored before they get to anything interesting.

Here is an example of how to narrow down your topic.

Example
Wide topic to narrow niche
Lose Weight   (wide topic)
Lose Weight diet   (just a little narrower)
Lose Weight Paleo Diet (more specific, getting better)
Lose Weight Paleo Diet for Teens (much more specific, includes who it targets)

The last one is the most specific. For Kindle books aimed at 15,000 to 20.000 words or so, the last one would be a very good and specific title. Try to make your title specific and include the major benefits.

Tools

Writing your book can be easier and a lot more fun if you use tools that make it easy. A tool can be an actual program or piece of software that makes writing easier, but it can also be a method or methodology.

It All Comes Clear In the Outline

Your book is going to be made up of chapters and sections. Those chapters and sections will make up the skeleton of your book, they are the frame that you will use to flesh out the whole thing.

The outline is one of the most important parts of the book in my opinion. If you do a good job with the outline, your book will have a good direction to go and grow. You can then block out writing the book into very small chunks. You can write those very small chunks at 15 minute intervals.

Not having a good outline will usually cause me to have many pauses in my writing. I will be thinking at the keyboard wondering what should go next. But a good outline sets the stage for success and allows me to use one of my favorite tools, that is the 15 minute time chunking method.

Time Chunking

When I have what I want to say broken down far enough with the outline, I can start writing the paragraphs and push for very good writing times. The very first draft I try to do very quickly, without a lot of analysis and without a lot of blending or any editing or rewriting.

Once the first draft is completed, then I begin the editing and the transitions into the next sections. It is during the second draft that I realize that I have forgotten something, or that I need to add something, or that I have to reword things so that they fit together seamlessly.

When I write I will set a 15 minute timer and I will make sure that I take a 5 minute or so break between each 15 minutes of writing time. For me, this method is invigorating. I see how much I get done, and it is so very encouraging. I keep a short log of how long I spend writing and how many words I write during that time. It has been surprising how much faster I am able to write now using this method than I was able to before I started using the time chunking.

The secret to the 15 minute time chunks is to eliminate all distractions. Close the door, turn off any other distractions, don't wander to Facebook or email.

For 15 minutes I will do nothing but write. I will let the words flow, and try to "splat" the words into the document. I just try to get the ideas down on paper so to speak. Then I stop after 15 minutes, stand up, take a break. I make a commitment to myself to focus completely on the writing, then do something completely different during the break. After 5 minutes I come back and set up another 15 minutes of uninterrupted writing.

I can write at least a thousand words per day. I strive for two thousand words per day, and sometimes exceed that. I can do it in an hour to an hour and a half of those 15 minute sprints. Just try it. If it doesn't fit your style then move on to something else. But this one method has helped me write while traveling, and during those short little times in between activities. I have trained myself to clear my mind and focus exclusively on the writing, because I know that 15 minutes isn't very long and I can go back to whatever else I was doing before the writing if I stay on task for those 15 minutes. I can only do this if I have an amazing outline. If the outline isn't detailed enough, then it takes more than 15 minutes just to come up to speed with where I left off.

Organization Tools

I like to use a mind map as a tool for getting my ideas into a logical organization. I first put my major ideas clustered around the central topic.

Then I add the sections and ideas that I want to talk about. Through this process the mind map grows. I start to rearrange the pieces, adding subsections and moving some to be underneath a different subtopic. I can often write the outline directly from the mind map. I use a free program called xMind, but there are a number of free mind map software packages out there. Find one that works for you.

The picture below shows what a mind map looks like.

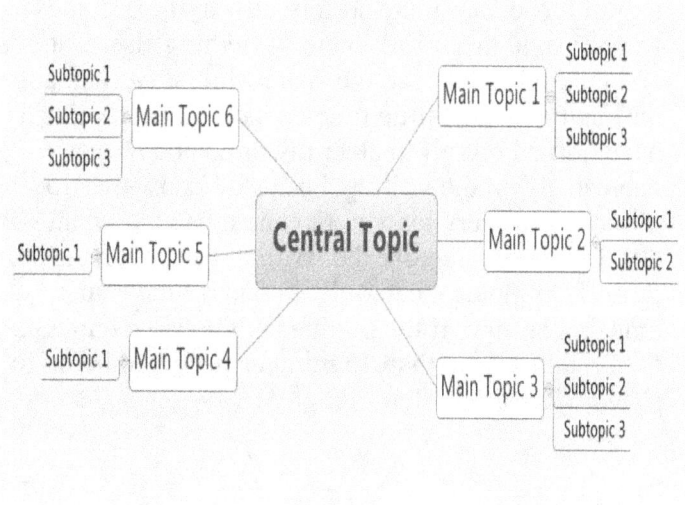

Figure 27 Mind Map

Writing Software

Many people use Microsoft Word as their word processor. I have put out a number of books using it. I like Microsoft Word, but I put my .doc or .docx documents through a converter called Kinstant Formatter to get them into Kindle format. You can read more about Kinstant Formatter here. http://incomenow.org/KinstantFormatter .

A different option is using Open Office Writer with the extension Writer2Epub. This option is free, and seems to do a good job. There are a lot of little nuances that Kindle wants you to have, and I have a hard time keeping them straight. The advantage of the Microsoft Word and the Kinstant Formatter is that all of the little details about the format are taken care of by the software. However, the Open Office solution is free.

I am now using Scrivener. Scrivener has extension for putting out documents that are formatted for Kindle, then using the same modules with different extensions to put out documents made for Createspace, for Barnes and Noble, and for Apple iTunes.

I love Scrivener. It lets you keep your research notes with the documents that you are writing. It is a tool for organizing your work as well as writing your books. It was well worth the cost.

By the way, I got a 20% discount. I wrote to Literature and Latte, the manufacturer of Scrivener and asked about any current coupons. They sent me back this:

I can offer you a coupon code that will give you a discount of 20% when you purchase a regular license for Scrivener via our web store at <http://www.getscrivener.com>. Just enter the code WORDSWITHJAM.

That's what I did, and I have been enjoying Scrivener ever since.

Modelling Success

I read lots of books and eBooks. I have lists of books that are my favorites and I go back to them again and again as references. However, I like to browse Amazon to see what non-fiction books are the most successful.

I open up Amazon.com, Select Kindle Store, and click Go on the search bar. Kindle bestsellers comes up on the left column. I select Kindle Best Sellers, then click on nonfiction. This is what the category column looks like then:

Amazon Best Sellers

Our most popular products based on sales. Updated hourly.

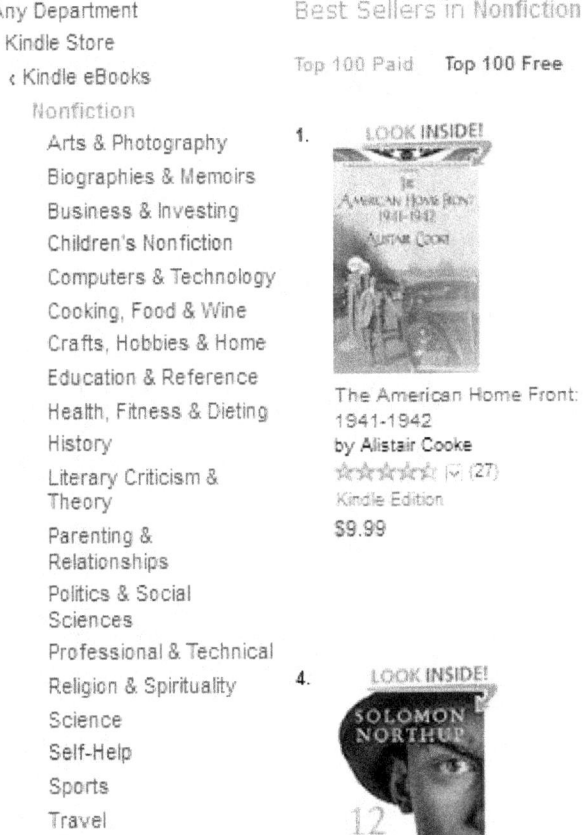

‹ Any Department
  ‹ Kindle Store
    ‹ Kindle eBooks
      Nonfiction
        Arts & Photography
        Biographies & Memoirs
        Business & Investing
        Children's Nonfiction
        Computers & Technology
        Cooking, Food & Wine
        Crafts, Hobbies & Home
        Education & Reference
        Health, Fitness & Dieting
        History
        Literary Criticism & Theory
        Parenting & Relationships
        Politics & Social Sciences
        Professional & Technical
        Religion & Spirituality
        Science
        Self-Help
        Sports
        Travel

Best Sellers in Nonfiction

Top 100 Paid   **Top 100 Free**

1. LOOK INSIDE!

The American Home Front: 1941-1942
by Alistair Cooke
★★★★★ ✓ (27)
Kindle Edition
$9.99

4. LOOK INSIDE!

Figure 27 Only The Non Fiction

Now, as I browse the books, my search has been narrowed to nonfiction books. I open up the ones that grab my attention, and if they have a sales rank of under 20,000, I feel like they are successful enough to model.

I take out a piece of paper or open up a document and I copy the table of contents of the book. I will write out the table of contents by hand on paper, or I will type out every word into my word processor. I NEVER use what I copy in anything that I am writing, but copying successful tables of contents gives me a chance to practice modeling a successful outline of someone else's book. I copy the table of contents from three books every day. Sometimes I will find a chapter title that will get me thinking, and I will have a new idea for a new book or a new chapter in something that I thought about writing.

This every day jump start to my creative processes is a tool that I believe makes a lot of difference in my writing. I will also copy one book description per day. Many of the book descriptions will have similar sections. Copying what other successful people do, prepares me to write my own book descriptions.

Model success. Take what seems to resonate with you and let go of the rest. Over time your writing will look more and more professional, because you will be thinking and communicating more and more like the professionals that you are modeling. You will always retain your own voice and style, they will just be colored by the exposure to what is really working.

eBook Publishing

Getting your book on Amazon is really pretty easy. Amazon has a guide for publishing your book. I don't want to reinvent the wheel, so here is the URL: https://kdp.amazon.com/help?topicId=A37Z49E2 DDQPP3 .

They have a free book that is a guide to getting your kindle book formatted.
http://www.amazon.com/dp/B007URVZJ6/ . I have already discussed how I use Microsoft Word and Kinstant Formatter (http://incomenow.org/KinstantFormatter) to publish mine. The important part is just get up and do it.

Spend a couple of days researching your proposed topic and put together a proposed title. Although I have spent most of this book trying to help you find what that title should look like, my experience is that the title of my book will change as I write it. So pick a title already and get started. As your book comes together, you will have more things to try and get into the title and it will evolve, getting better and better. Then go through the steps and get the book up on Amazon.

eBook Marketing

Marketing is both straight forward and also very complex. Here are the tips that seem to make the most difference in getting my book sold.

1. Give the book a couple of days after publishing it before doing anything to promote it. Make sure you can find the book on Amazon, and capture the URL. The URL is going to be something very big, like this: http://www.amazon.com/Write-Step---Step-Book-Bestsellers-ebook/dp/B00I0MKFVY/ . You can shorten the URL by eliminating everything after the .com/ to the db, like this: http://www.amazon.com/dp/B00I0MKFVY/ . The KDP bookshelf also has a link called Store Links, this link will give you the same compressed link as above, the one above being an example of the US link. Be sure to cut and paste the URL into a browser to make sure that your book comes up when the URL is entered. This short URL is the one that you will use on twitter, Facebook, on blogs or webpages, and is the one you will send to any contractors that help you promote your book.

2. If you have done a good job with the niche, the title, the categories, the search terms, and the cover, you should start seeing a few sales. My suggestion is to drop the price to 99 cents for the first week. Join the Facebook groups that I list for you in the resources pages, and watch for people that are looking for 99 cent buy swaps.

That basically means you will buy their 99 cent book, and they will buy yours. Ask them for a book review, and be very generous with reviews of other people's books, especially those that are on free promotion.

Ask friends and family to purchase the book at 99 cents and ask them for reviews. Tell them that the price of the book is going up to $2.99 shortly.

3. When you have five to seven good reviews, set up a free KDP give away day and boost the price to $2.99.

The KDP Select Free days don't work just by themselves like they used to. They need a little bit of a jump start. I have provided a list of sites that will feature your free day promotion in the resources section in the back of this book. I prefer buying a gig on Fiverr.com that will submit the book on these sites for me.

Here are three Gigs that have worked for me. I like the first one best. I will usually buy the gig extra where they feature my book in their daily newsletter.

http://fiverr.com/bknights/submit-your-free-kindle-book-to-the-15-best-kindle-promotion-sites

http://fiverr.com/timmybx/manually-submit-your-kdp-kindle-ebook-free-day-promo-to-15-kindle-book-sites

http://fiverr.com/thedesertgirl/submit-your-free-kindle-book-to-12-promo-sites

4. Schedule your free day and your gig to promote your book on the free day. ONLY USE ONE FREE DAY. I'll show you why later. Also announce your free day, on the free day, on each of the Facebook groups.

Track everything. Keep track of how many books are being downloaded. Also ask for reviews during your free day on the Facebook groups.

One other trick that seems to help a lot is to stop the free promotion about 5:00pm, just a few hours before it would end normally. There is still a lot of downloading going on at that time, and you could get a dozen or two sales over night. Be sure to record the sales rank and the category rankings early in the morning, and throughout the next day. These could be at their temporary best ranking for a while. If your book makes it to the #1 or #2 spot for a category, you will likely see improved sales while the book stays at those spots.

5. Get your calendar down and circle the free day, then count 18 days later and circle that day. Do it again three more times. You should have 5 circled days in 90 days. You can do one free day every 18 days during your 90 KDP term. If you use different Fiverr vendors to post your free days you can keep this pace up. I have a book that gets 12+ sales every time I run a promotion like this, and the book sells two or three times more books for the next week or more if it can stay in the top 5 or so for a category.

This is totally individual per book however. I have other books that only sell six to ten copies during a promotion like this. That still brings me back more than I put out with a $5 Fiverr gig, but the return on investment isn't nearly as good as my other books. Just track your results and make sure that each promotion brings in more than it costs.

6. Over time get your book announced in the book promotion websites I provide in the resources page. This part takes time and brings in customers a few at a time.

7. Write more books! Each and every book is a salesman for your other books. Re-publish your Kindle books with a link in the back pointing to your other books that are all related. If you put out a book that is successful, design five more titles around the same topic, because people that like your writing and like a specific topic will often buy all of the ones you put out about that topic.

8. Find something in your niche that you can give away for email addresses. Start creating your own email list, and let them know when your next book comes out.

9. Start a blog about your topic. Put informational things in each blog post, and feature a picture of your book about the subject on one of the side columns.

10. Use keyword and article marketing concepts to get your blogposts ranked in Google.

You can get more information about using Google Keyword Planner to help you do this from another book that I wrote.
http://www.amazon.com/dp/B00E45ADKE/.

11. Have fun. Just enjoy the writing and promoting as it goes along. I was watching the figure skating competition from the 2014 Winter Olympics. One of the commentators said that a French skater had been having difficulties. Then her mother told her to just skate for the joy of skating. That seemed to turn everything around and she was suddenly putting in her best performances of the season. So apply that to yourself. Just write for the joy of writing, and see how much more fun creating books can be.

Conclusion

Your best chance of producing a book that will sell is to model it after the successful books on Amazon. I have given you the tools, the sites, and the methods for coming up with tons of successful topics and subtopics to write about. Those same sites can act as repositories for the information that you will need to fill your book with, but make sure that you present the information with your own style and voice. Write your book as if you were talking to a friend. Only include the things that you think would interest your personal friend.

Make a goal of how many books you plan to write, and how often you have to publish to keep up with that goal. Break down the goal into how many words you have to write per day, and strive to meet your goal. Write for the joy of writing, and enjoy the journey as you experience it. Most everything else will fall into place as you do. Don't put it off any longer. Pull out your research paper and start now by putting that research to work and start writing your book.

If you enjoyed this book, please leave a review on the Amazon website. Reviews are so important to the success of self-published books. You can leave a review here:

https://www.amazon.com/review/create-review?ie=UTF8&asin=B00IODSNVI

Here is to your Ultimate Success,

Dean Giles

Connect with me
Email: dean@incomenow.com
Blog: http://incomenow.com
Facebook:
https://www.facebook.com/WriteAStepByStepBoo
k
Sign up for my email list:
http://incomenow.org/writing

Appendix

Thank you for reading the book!

If you enjoyed this book, please leave a Review.

https://www.amazon.com/review/create-review?ie=UTF8&asin=B00IODSNVI.

Reviews help so much! Thank you in advance.

Dean R. Giles

About the Author

Dean R. Giles has been an avid reader his entire life. He preferred reading to doing homework through a lot of his school years. Writing became part of his work through every job that he had.

He has contributed to numerous technical manuals, information products, and detailed reports over the years. Story telling was a favorite activity with his children over a number of years.

Writing books became a natural extension of various interests. He began studying writing in the late 2000s and began publishing books in 2011.

If you have any feedback, questions, or just want to drop me a note, you can send an email to dean@austinsgift.com .

Find out about my upcoming Fantasy novel at Austinsgift.com/magic.

<u>Other Books by This Author:</u>

About Writing

How to Steal Like an Author:
http://www.amazon.com/dp/B00NVN99FK
Discover Book Ideas:
http://www.amazon.com/dp/B00IODSNVI
Write On
http://www.amazon.com/dp/B00O9LIBMK

Not About Writing

Dragons Restored
http://www.amazon.com/dp/B014N2E9CU
Life's Poetry
http://www.amazon.com/dp/B00UU0UQ2C
The Snow Birthday
http://www.amazon.com/dp/B00BWAP6SS
Summer Time Fun
http://www.amazon.com/dp/B00DZVYG4W
Keyword Planner
http://www.amazon.com/dp/B00E45ADKE

Connect with me

Email: dean@autstinsgift.com
Blog: http://austinsgift.com
Facebook:
https://www.facebook.com/DragonsRestored/
 Sign up for my email list: http://austinsgift.com/writing

Facebook Book Groups

https://www.facebook.com/groups/426282137432533/
https://www.facebook.com/groups/389343847782037/
https://www.facebook.com/groups/pageoneprofits/
https://www.facebook.com/groups/BooksLuvers/
https://www.facebook.com/groups/abrex/

https://www.facebook.com/groups/passionforbooks/

https://www.facebook.com/groups/childrenbookclub/

https://www.facebook.com/groups/Bookjunkiesfreebies/

https://www.facebook.com/groups/bookplace/

https://www.facebook.com/groups/freetoday/

https://www.facebook.com/groups/270558336379692/

https://www.facebook.com/groups/157960580960255/

https://www.facebook.com/groups/memberswritersgroup/

https://www.facebook.com/groups/469592073074586/

https://www.facebook.com/groups/KidBooksWithGoodValues/

https://www.facebook.com/groups/AmazonBookClubs/

https://www.facebook.com/groups/187547284642012/

https://www.facebook.com/groups/booknest/

https://www.facebook.com/groups/174224899314282/

https://www.facebook.com/groups/623206594363552/

https://www.facebook.com/groups/ebooksrock/

https://www.facebook.com/groups/kindlemojo/

https://www.facebook.com/groups/2204546223/

https://www.facebook.com/groups/204725947524/

https://www.facebook.com/groups/booksgoneviral/

https://www.facebook.com/groups/iluvbooks/

https://www.facebook.com/groups/2204565182/

https://www.facebook.com/groups/3203569747321
42/
https://www.facebook.com/groups/1794940688200
33/
https://www.facebook.com/groups/bookjunkiepro
motions/
https://www.facebook.com/groups/4364029664391
26/
https://www.facebook.com/groups/freebkrus/
https://www.facebook.com/groups/boomdom/
https://www.facebook.com/groups/370900356880/
https://www.facebook.com/groups/kindlemarketin
grevelations/
https://www.facebook.com/groups/ParaYourAbno
rmalAuthors/
https://www.facebook.com/groups/FreeTodayOnA
mazon/
https://www.facebook.com/groups/ReviewersRoun
dup/
https://www.facebook.com/groups/9476163038/
https://www.facebook.com/groups/freeebooks/
https://www.facebook.com/groups/1402168653333
862/

Places to Post Your Kindle Select
Free Days

http://ereadernewstoday.com/ent-free-book-
submissions/

http://www.fkbooksandtips.com/for-authors/free-kindle-book-submission-form/
http://digitalbooktoday.com/12-top-100-submit-your-free-book-to-be-included-on-this-list/
http://indiebookoftheday.com/authors/free-on-kindle-listing/
http://rastephensonauthor.blogspot.com/p/free-promotion-for-independent-authors.html
http://www.mybookandmycoffee.com/p/free-ebook-feature.html
http://freedigitalreads.com/author-submissions/
http://indieauthorbookreviews.wordpress.com/kindle-promo/
http://www.sevenbillionreaderbooks.com/free-kindle-book-submission/
http://www.pixelofink.com/sfkb/
http://bargainebookhunter.com/free-book-notification-form/
http://kindlenationdaily.com/kindle-nation-daily-free-and-bargain-book-listings/
http://www.freebooksifter.com/?c=7
http://www.dailyfreebooks.co.uk/promote-your-kindle-book.html
http://onehundredfreebooks.com/author-free-kindle-book-submission.html
http://www.ebookxp.net/submit.php
http://www.totallyfreestuff.com/submit.asp?m=0
http://www.icravefreebies.com/contact/
http://bargainebookhunter.com/feature-your-book/
http://addictedtoebooks.com/free#comment-3747
http://ebookshabit.com/for-authors/
http://www.theereadercafe.com/p/authors.html
http://www.freebookdude.com/p/list-your-free-book.html

http://www.frugal-freebies.com/p/submit-freebie.html

Facebook Pages to List Free Books On

These are quick and easy, just go to the pages on your free day, and put a link to your Kindle eBook in the post. They appear immediately.

https://www.facebook.com/Freebies4Mom
https://www.facebook.com/bookskindle
https://www.facebook.com/FreeBookFeed
https://www.facebook.com/KindleUtopia
https://www.facebook.com/pages/Free-Daily-eBooks/277545182364423
https://www.facebook.com/FreeEbooksDownloads
https://www.facebook.com/eReaderLove
https://www.facebook.com/KindleFreebies
https://www.facebook.com/ePublish.a.Book
https://www.facebook.com/pages/Free-Kindle-Books-Updated-Daily/155923931093850
https://www.facebook.com/ourawesomegang

Places to Advertise Your Book

http://www.goodreads.com/
http://www.booktalk.com/authors/
http://www.kindleboards.com/
http://www.librarything.com/
http://www.authonomy.com/?from=bookarmy
http://www.booktalk.org/
http://www.booksie.com/
http://www.wattpad.com/
http://www.shelfari.com/
http://www.nothingbinding.com/
http://www.jacketflap.com/
http://www.whowrotewhat.net/
http://www.timgreatonforum.blogspot.ca/
http://www.writers.net/
http://www.bibliophil.org/
http://www.bookbrowse.com/
http://www.bookbuzzr.com/
http://www.filedby.com/
http://www.bookhitch.com/
http://savvybookwriters.wordpress.com/
http://www.bookreportradio.com/
http://www.timgreatonforum.blogspot.ca/
http://www.bowkerlink.com/
http://www.kindlemojo.com
http://blog.booksontheknob.org
http://addictedtoebooks.com/submission/
http://freebooksy.com/about/

Bibliography and More Resources

Giles, Dean, *Keyword Planner: How to Exploit Google Adwords Keyword Planner to Get Unlimited, Buyer-Targeted, Long-Tail Key*words,
http://www.amazon.com/dp/B00E45ADKE/

Giles, Dean, *Write a Step-by-Step Book*,
http://www.amazon.com/dp/B00I0MKFVY/

Aaron, Rachel, *2,000 to 10,000: Writing Faster, Writing Better, Writing More Of What You Love*,
http://www.amazon.com/2k-10k-Writing-Faster-Better-ebook/dp/B009NKXAWS/

Allen, Christopher David, *How to Publish a #1 Best Seller On Kindle – No Cost Publishing and Marketing Secrets of a Bestselling Author – How to Book and Guide for Smart Dummies*,
http://www.amazon.com/HOW-PUBLISH-BEST-SELLER-KINDLE-ebook/dp/B0089TESCU/

Becker, Dennis, *One Problem Product Creation*,
http://incomenow.org/one-problem-ebook

Covey, Steven R., *7 Habits of Highly Effective People: Powerful Lessons in Personal Change*,
http://www.amazon.com/Habits-Highly-Effective-People-Anniversary-ebook/dp/B00GOZV3TM/

Drum, Deb and Harrop, Amy, *Description Detective 2*, http://incomenow.org/description-detective2

Eagle, Dennis and Villegas, Oliver, *7 Secret Steps to Best Selling Author*, http://www.amazon.com/Secret-Steps-Bestselling-Author-Revealed-ebook/dp/B00EA1XGJW/

Kindle Direct Publishing, *Building Your Book for Kindle*, http://www.amazon.com/Building-Your-Kindle-Direct-Publishing-ebook/dp/B007URVZJ6/

Locke, John, *How I Sold 1 Million eBooks in 5 Months*, http://www.amazon.com/How-Sold-Million-eBooks-Months-ebook/dp/B0056BMK6K/

Redwine, Kate, *Crush It With Kindle Publishing The Entrepreneur's Guide for Self Publishing Books on Kindle, and Promoting Your Book to #1 Bestseller Status*, http://www.amazon.com/Publishing-Entrepreneurs-Building-Promoting-Bestseller-ebook/dp/B00DH8STT6/

Rofe, Rachel, KInstant Formatter, http://incomenow.org/KinstantFormatter

Kleon, Austin, *Steal Like an Artist: 10 Things No One Told You About Creativity*, http://www.amazon.com/Steal-Like-Artist-Things-Creative-ebook/dp/B0074QGGK6/

LJS Quote 2 Motivate, *Quotes For Writers: Inspiration, Advice, Humor, and Motivational Stories From Famous Authors*, http://www.amazon.com/Quotes-Writers-Inspiration-Motivational-Stories-ebook/dp/B00HFA4V9O/

Plat, Sean and Truant, Johnny B., *Write. Publish. Repeat.*, http://www.amazon.com/Publish-Repeat-No-Luck-Required-Self-Publishing-Success-ebook/dp/B00H26IFJS/

Scott, Steve, *How to Discover Bestselling eBook Ideas – The Bulletproof Strategy*, http://www.amazon.com/Discover-Best-Selling-Nonfiction-eBook-Ideas-ebook/dp/B009D6JL2O/

Tardif, Cheryl Kaye, *How I Made $42,000 In One Month Selling My Kindle eBooks*, http://www.amazon.com/Made-Month-Selling-Kindle-eBooks-ebook/dp/B0080USSYW/

Turner, Laina, *All I Know About eBook Marketing*, http://www.amazon.com/All-Know-About-e-Book-Marketing-ebook/dp/B009VO9YGW/

Vulich, Nick, *Freeking Idiots Guide to Writing a Kindle Bestseller Tips and Tricks to Make Your Book a Bestseller in Its Category*, http://www.amazon.com/Freaking-Writing-Bestseller-bestseller-category-ebook/dp/B00B1Z7YFM/

Williams, Glyn, *Bestseller Tactics: Advanced Self Publishing Techniques to Help You Sell More Books On Amazon and Make More Money. Advanced Author Marketing.*
http://www.amazon.com/Bestseller-Tactics-publishing-techniques-Marketing-ebook/dp/B00GHTL5O8/

Free eBooks That You Can Download

How to Write Book Descriptions:
http://incomenow.org/reports/book-descriptions.pdf

Are you too busy earning a living to make any real money? http://bit.ly/15WMoWJ